sharks

priddy books
big ideas for little people

what is a shark?

Sharks take water in and pump it out through their gill slits.

Excellent eyesight

Nostrils—sharks have a very good sense of smell

Mouth filled with lots of sharp teeth

Pectoral fin

Sharks are a type of fish that have existed since before the dinosaurs. They can be scary and extremely dangerous, but are among the most incredible creatures on Earth.

There are more than 300 different types of sharks, and they are found in oceans all over the world. They come in many shapes and sizes, from the size of your arm to some that are bigger than a bus!

Dorsal fins

Caudal fin

Anal fin

Pelvic fin

The great white is most people's idea of a "killer shark." They are large, fearsome predators, and although they have attacked people, a great white would much rather eat a seal or sea lion!

This shark's teeth are razor-sharp, jagged, and arranged in rows. Like in all sharks, when a tooth breaks off, another one moves into its place.

Skin covered in denticles—very rough, sharp scales

Great white shark

Large black eyes, with very good eyesight

There are few scarier sights than a shark's dorsal fin on the water surface.

Scarred skin, caused by unfortunate prey fighting back

The great white can have as many as 3,000 razor-sharp teeth.

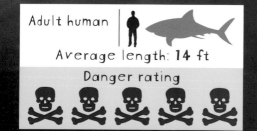

Adult human

Average length: **14 ft**

Danger rating

Hammerhead shark

The shape of its head helps the hammerhead steer itself in the water.

These sharks live in the coastal parts of warm, tropical oceans.

This shark has an unusually wide, hammer-shaped head. Its eyes are on each side of its head, and its first dorsal fin is very large and pointed. This weird-looking shark has very good senses for finding prey.

Average length: 11 ft

Danger rating

Tiger shark

Tiger sharks get their name from the striped markings along their sides. They will eat almost anything, and given the chance, will attack any people nearby.

Tiger sharks have been found with cans, bottles, and other garbage in their stomachs!

Average length: 10 ft

Danger rating

whale shark

Every whale shark has a unique pattern of spots.

Huge mouth, up to 4 feet wide

Average length: 26 ft

Danger rating

Whale sharks use their entire bodies, not just their fins, to swim.

Whale sharks
can live to be
150 years old.

On its tail, the
top fin is much
larger than the
lower fin.

The magnificent whale shark is the largest
shark (and the largest fish) in the world.
It uses its very large mouth to filter
out plankton from the sea to eat.

It is a slow-moving, gentle giant and is
harmless to people. Whale sharks have
distinctive spotted and striped markings
all over their very rough and thick skin.

This shark, also called the ragged-tooth shark, is not actually as scary as it looks. Sand tiger sharks spend most of their time slowly swimming around reefs and wrecks, feeding on squid and slippery fish, which their teeth are designed to catch.

Sand tiger sharks gulp air and then burp to control their buoyancy!

Sand tiger shark

Blue shark

This beautiful, fast-swimming shark is prized by fishermen around the world.

This shark is also known as the blue dog, or blue whaler shark.

Blue sharks are found in the deep waters of oceans all over the world, where they often form large groups, or "schools" of sharks. They are long and sleek with a pointed snout, and are fast swimmers. Their name comes from the distinctive purple-blue color of their skin.

Average length: 12 ft

Danger rating

Basking sharks are huge but have very tiny, almost useless teeth. Like the whale shark, it filters its food out of the water using gill rakers. Also called sunfish, they spend most of their time close to the water surface, basking in the sun.

Very rough skin

Gill rakers filter food from the water.

Average length: 23 ft

Danger rating

Basking shark

Of all sharks, mako sharks are the fastest swimmers. They can reach speeds of over 30 mph and leap high out of the water. Fishermen like to catch makos, but are often bitten when they reel them in!

Large, black eyes

The razor-sharp teeth are long and smooth.

Mako shark

Wobbegong shark

Average length: 6 ft
Danger rating

Spotted pattern skin

Long, flat, and flexible body

The wobbegong shark's unusual markings help to keep them hidden in the coral reefs in which they live.

Wobbegongs are nocturnal, and rest on the sea bed in the day. They are not aggressive, but if disturbed they will give a very nasty bite and will not let go!

Nurse shark

Nurse sharks use whisker-like organs called barbels to touch and taste for food on the sea bed.

Average length: 6 ft

Danger rating

Unlike most sharks, their skin is smooth.

These slow-moving sharks feed on shellfish on the sea bed, where they use their strong pectoral fins to "walk" through the sand. Nurse sharks will not attack unless they are disturbed, but have a very powerful, crushing bite.

Reef shark

This blacktip reef shark is one of the most common sharks in the world. It lives around coral reefs in the Indian and Pacific Oceans. It is fairly harmless, but has been known to bite people wading in shallow water.

Blunt, rounded snout

Like most sharks, they have lighter skin underneath.

Named after the black tips on the ends of its fins.

Average length: 6 ft

Danger rating

The bull shark is the type of shark that attacks people most often. This is mainly because it lives in shallow, coastal areas. They are the only sharks that can live in fresh water, and have been found many miles inland up the Amazon River in South America.

Average length: 7 ft
Danger rating

Large first dorsal fin

Large, stocky, bull-like body

Short, blunt snout

This fish is scavenging for scraps of food.

Small eyes

Bull shark

whitetip shark

Whitetip sharks are known to follow pilot whales, looking for food.

Very large, white-tipped dorsal fin

Stocky, powerful body

Large groups of oceanic whitetips have been known to attack people stranded in the water after shipwrecks and air crashes. They are deep-sea sharks, and migrate over long distances.

Rays are closely related to sharks. The giant manta ray is the largest type and can grow to 30 feet wide. It is harmless to people, but a blow from one of its "wings" would certainly pack a fearsome punch!

Huge pectoral fins or wings

Gill slits

Fins used to funnel food into its mouth.

Long tail

Average length: 22 ft
Danger rating

Manta ray

Stingrays live in the warm, tropical parts of the Atlantic Ocean and Caribbean, where they feed almost constantly. They have poisonous spines in their tails, which they use to defend themselves against predators—mainly sharks!

Stinging spine in tail

Eyes on top of its head

A stingray's tail can be twice as long as its body.

Its sharp stinger may break off into a victim's wound but will regrow.

Stingray